madonna

HER STORY (FORMERLY LUCKY STAR) BY MICHAEL McKENZIE

BOBCAT
BOOKS

LONDON · NEW YORK · SYDNEY · COLOGNE

© 1985 Michael McKenzie
First published 1985 by Columbus
Books, London. This edition © 1987
Bobcat Books (A Division of Book
Sales Ltd)

Book Designed by Martin L.
Burgoyne

Exclusive distributors:
Book Sales Limited
8/9 Frith Street.
London W1V 5TZ, UK.

Music Sales Corporation
24 East 22nd Street, New York.
NY 10010, USA.

Omnibus Press
GPO Box 3304, Sydney.
NSW 2001, Australia.

To the Music Trade only
Music Sales Limited
8/9 Frith Street.
London W1V 5TZ, UK.

Picture credits: Beth Baptiste,
Peter Cunningham, Edo Bertoglio.
Deborah Feingold, Dan Gilroy,
Marcus Leatherdale, Laura Levine.
Stephen Lewicki, Curtis Knapp.
Michael McKenzie, Patrick
McCullum, Detroit Chamber of
Commerce, John Sex. Haoui
Montag, LFI.

ISBN 0.7119.1181.9
Order No. BOB 10088

CONTENTS

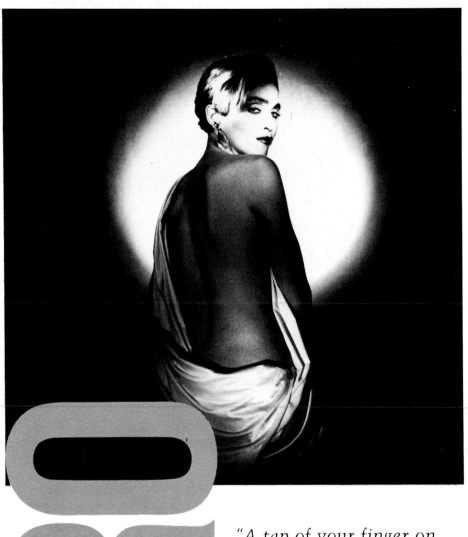

INTRO

> "*A tap of your finger on the drum fires all the sounds and starts a new harmony.*"

Arthur Rimbaud,
Illuminations

The pop music industry is notorious for inventing new heroes, the momentary stars who flare up on the pages of glossy magazines, then flicker and fade like a paper flame. Who among us does not own a record, purchased within the past few years, which raises the embarrassing question: "Did I really, of my own free will, pay money for this?"

But occasionally you find a great album, one whose songs seem to get better with each listening. And as time passes, the album reminds you of where you were then, who you loved, what you were doing, and what you were dreaming. Then all the time and money spent on those godforsaken albums seem insignificant. For in the light of really magical music, the little blemishes of life disappear.

It is not often that an album comes along that can electrify the radio airwaves. The Beatles, the Stones, and David Bowie had that magic, the power to make songs more than just music. And now there is Madonna, swaying through our minds with a message of holidays, lucky stars, virgins, angels, and physical attraction. Magic.

In the late seventies and early eighties, the phenomena of breakdancing and graffiti art began lighting up the street life of America's great cities. Madonna was there, flowing with the downtown action, enhancing the scene with her own talent, putting it all on the line with her interpretations. Her unique blend of Latin good looks, dance training, street smarts, and Motown roots, combined with a burning desire for success, has taken her to the top of the entertainment business.

It is no surprise to those of us who know Madonna that she has succeeded in both music and movies. She is an incredibly visual person and has attracted New York's best upcoming visual artists since her first day there.

The pictures you see in this book document Madonna's rise to superstardom as seen through the eyes of some of New York's most talented young photographers: Beth Baptiste, Peter Cunningham, Deborah Feingold, Edo Bertoglio, Marcus Leatherdale, Patrick

McMullan, and Curtis Knapp. Remember their names, for you will no doubt be seeing their work on album covers for many years to come.

This book follows the pulse of one of America's most important young stars, chronicling her rise from the back streets of Detroit and New York to story-book stardom. It is a story about poverty, love, passion, desire, and fame. It is the story of Madonna Louise Ciccone, a girl whose life is a map of hope and determination.

Lucky Star is an American success story.

...like a

virgin

T he 1950s witnessed the birth of rock & roll in America, the coming of Elvis in a post-war society that worshiped beautiful girls, hot cars, and weekends. As the fifties gave way to the sixties, America was at the height of a nonstop dance craze, and the musical soul of the dance scene was Detroit, Michigan—better known as Motown, U.S.A. Big, fast cars and red-hot music were the two products that Motown was cranking out with furious efficiency. And while the "monster motors" of Detroit made their reputation as the world's fastest and most powerful cars, Berry Gordy, the genius/owner of Motown Records made his own mark on the rock & roll world.

It was 1959—a year that found several of America's more flamboyant teen idols in strange circumstances: Elvis Presley was in, of all places, the army; Mr. Rock & Roll, Chuck Berry, was in jail; Little Richard quit the rock fold to become a Baptist minister; Buddy Holly, only 23 years old, died in a plane crash.

On August 16, 1959, in Rochester, Michigan, just a shoo-bee-doo down the road from Motown headquarters, Madonna Louise Ciccone was born. Her father, an engineer for the Chrysler Corporation, named his first daughter Madonna after her mother, a fairly typical gesture for an Italian-American family. And if her name seemed intriguing and unusual, there was little to indicate just how intriguing and unusual the young Madonna would eventually become.

The Ciccones were a large family (five boys and three girls). All five of Madonna Louise's brothers were born before her, but both of her sisters are younger than she is.

When Madonna was six, her mother lost a battle with cancer and the Ciccones became a one-parent family. Although the tragedy took its emotional toll on Madonna, the event also served to draw her closer to her father. Later, Madonna was to dedicate her first album to her dad.

"I had a musical up for a year, but I quit father to let me take

detroit

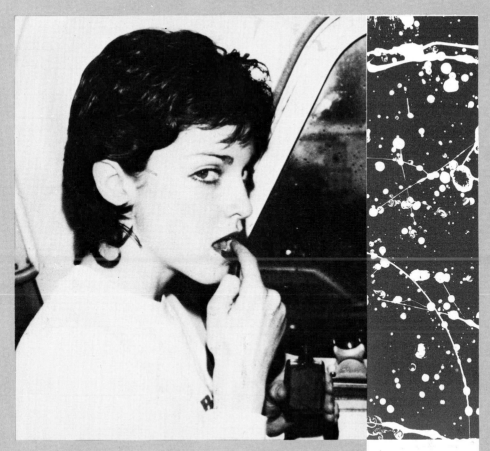

bringing. I studied piano and convinced my ballet lessons instead."

Some two years after the death of her mother, Madonna was in for another parental surprise: Her father announced that he would be remarrying, and the new mom was none other than the family's housekeeper. The transition was awkward for the eight-year-old Madonna, and the relationship can be summarized by her recollection that "I remember it being really hard for me to get the word 'mother' out of my mouth. It was really painful."

With "another woman" now in her father's life, Madonna started looking elsewhere for attention. The family's backyard soon served as a pubescent discotheque, and in the competitive environment of an eight-child household, Madonna's early bouncing to the sounds of Motown

The highlight of the flick came when an egg was fried on Madonna's stomach.

made her the talk of the household, if not yet the town. Daddy's little girl, still a few years away from the legitimate teeny-bopper age of thirteen, was already hot on the dance floor.

"I had a musical upbringing," Madonna has recalled of her childhood years. "I studied piano for a year but I quit and convinced my father to let me take ballet lessons instead." All five of Madonna's brothers played musical instruments; some appeared in high school plays, and two even attempted musical careers. Madonna was the only one in her family to devote her attention to dance, however.

Because her family had moved several times, Madonna was forced to pinball her way through three Catholic schools as a child: St. Andrews, St. Fredricks, and the Sacred Heart Academy. Whatever humor she has doled out to the press about her Catholic upbringing, she has, in more retrospective moments, noted that the religious schooling helped her develop a sense of self-discipline.

It was that very discipline, combined with no lack of confidence, that helped Madonna achieve unlimited success while her competitors disappeared into the maze of What-Was-The-Name-of-That-Band-Land. "I felt a lot of affection for them," Madonna has said of the myriad New Wave bands who were early eighties competition. "But I only thought that a handful of them were going on to any success. I thought," she summarized, "that they were all lazy."

Of all the things Madonna has been accused of, laziness has never been one of them. By her own estimation, she comes across as "someone who knows what they want. So if that's what you mean by tough, maybe that's what people think of me." Yes, Madonna will be called tough—tough, aggressive, self-centered, and a catalog of descriptive phrases not fit for print. Her admirers—and her detractors—seem to grow exponentially on a daily basis, but despite all odds, there is one thing on which everyone agrees: Madonna Louise Ciccone is a star. And, like a shooting star, Madonna's movement toward success has been substantially faster than those around her, leaving many acquaintances light years behind.

Madonna's first starring role in film occurs not in the spring Orion film **Desperately Seeking Susan**, but in a production substantially less lofty. Shot in 1972, the film was a super-8 short directed by one of her eighth-grade classmates. Although it never received the attention of Hollywood, history will record that the highlight of the flick came when an egg was fried on Madonna's stomach. What this means in human terms is that Madonna, even in eighth grade, knew how to get the cameras on her—with a vengeance.

Much has been made of Madonna's statement that "From the start, I was a bad girl," but no one short of a twelfth-century monk would view her in those terms. Her teachers and neighbors from Detroit think of Madonna, and her entire family for that matter, as "lovely people and fine neighbors." In grade school and high school, Madonna excelled in both the artistic and the academic courses she took. In fact, when she graduated from Rochester Adams High School in 1976, her academic grade point average combined with her skills in dance and theatre won her a full scholarship to the University of Michigan.

In high school, Madonna gave clear indications of what was to come. By age sixteen, she had made her mark in the Rochester Adams theater department. Madonna worked her way up the thespian ladder, ultimately landing lead roles in several school plays. Her forte, unsurprisingly, was musicals, since she could fully utilize her dance training in that context. It was only high school, but Madonna was already a star.

Upon graduation, Madonna, the little girl from Rochester, gyrated her seventeen-year-old body into the University of Michigan dance department. From her short and spiky punk haircut to her ripped and safety-pinned leotards, Madonna did everything she could to call attention to herself, which put off the majority of her conservative ballerina peers. Little Madonna Ciccone, all 5'4" of her, did indeed call a lot of attention to herself—and attracted her fair share of jealousy at the same time.

As you might expect, Madonna is not the kind of girl who's likely to fall head over heels for a University of Michigan jock, and she didn't. In fact, the one memorable beau she did have from her college days is none other than Steve Bray, the very talented drummer who co-wrote "Angel," "Over and Over," "Pretender," and "Stay" on the **Like a Virgin** album.

Bray was a waiter at the Blue Frogge, a University of Michigan nightclub where Madonna used to go and dance the night away. Madonna fell for the tall, black, and handsome Bray like a ton of bricks.

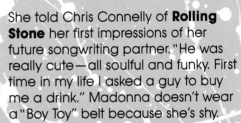

She told Chris Connelly of **Rolling Stone** her first impressions of her future songwriting partner. "He was really cute—all soulful and funky. First time in my life I asked a guy to buy me a drink." Madonna doesn't wear a "Boy Toy" belt because she's shy.

Madonna's stay at the University of Michigan, four-year scholarship notwithstanding, proved short fused. After a year as a dance major, Madonna angled her sultry self to the Big Apple, landing in New York's notorious Times Square with $35 in her pocket. Curiously, Madonna's flight from the safe ivory tower of Michigan University to the dark streets of New York City was spurred by none other than her ballet teacher. "He was constantly putting all that stuff about New York in my ear," Madonna has said. "I was hesitant, and my father and everyone were against it, but he really said, 'Go for it.' "

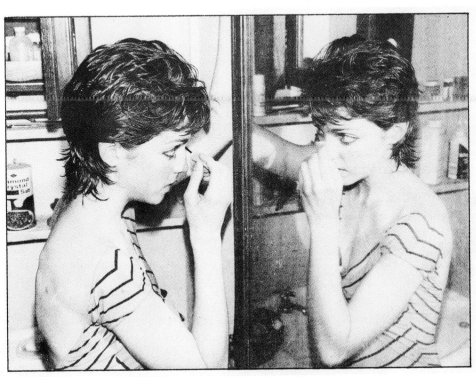

Madonna circa 1978, making up before hitting the club circuit.

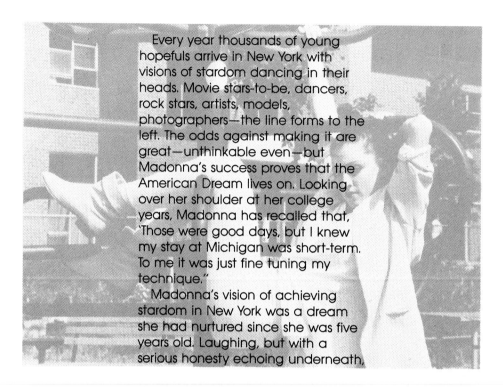

Every year thousands of young hopefuls arrive in New York with visions of stardom dancing in their heads. Movie stars-to-be, dancers, rock stars, artists, models, photographers—the line forms to the left. The odds against making it are great—unthinkable even—but Madonna's success proves that the American Dream lives on. Looking over her shoulder at her college years, Madonna has recalled that, 'Those were good days, but I knew my stay at Michigan was short-term. To me it was just fine tuning my technique."

Madonna's vision of achieving stardom in New York was a dream she had nurtured since she was five years old. Laughing, but with a serious honesty echoing underneath,

"Dance means freedom. Moving your body to music is the ultimate release."

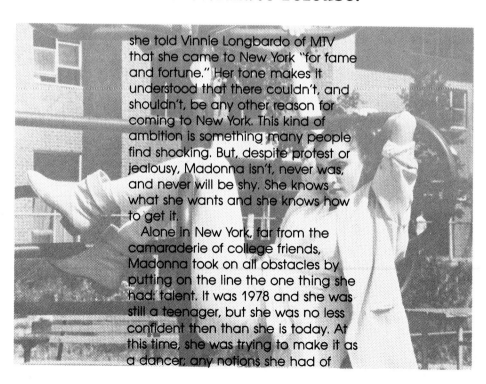

she told Vinnie Longbardo of MTV that she came to New York "for fame and fortune." Her tone makes it understood that there couldn't, and shouldn't, be any other reason for coming to New York. This kind of ambition is something many people find shocking. But, despite protest or jealousy, Madonna isn't, never was, and never will be shy. She knows what she wants and she knows how to get it.

Alone in New York, far from the camaraderie of college friends, Madonna took on all obstacles by putting on the line the one thing she had: talent. It was 1978 and she was still a teenager, but she was no less confident then than she is today. At this time, she was trying to make it as a dancer; any notions she had of

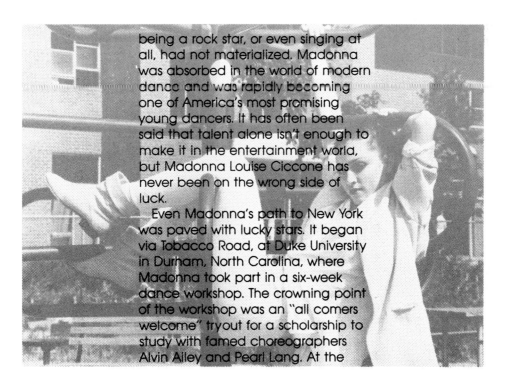

being a rock star, or even singing at all, had not materialized. Madonna was absorbed in the world of modern dance and was rapidly becoming one of America's most promising young dancers. It has often been said that talent alone isn't enough to make it in the entertainment world, but Madonna Louise Ciccone has never been on the wrong side of luck.

Even Madonna's path to New York was paved with lucky stars. It began via Tobacco Road, at Duke University in Durham, North Carolina, where Madonna took part in a six-week dance workshop. The crowning point of the workshop was an "all comers welcome" tryout for a scholarship to study with famed choreographers Alvin Ailey and Pearl Lang. At the

When my father came to visit, he was mortified. The place was crawling with cockroaches. There were winos in the hallways, and the entire place smelled like stale beer."

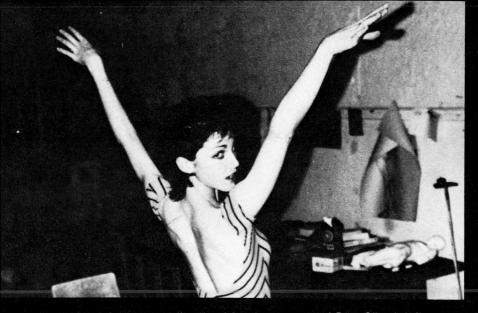

Madonna takes an over-the-shoulder dance pose at Dan Gilroy's loft.

audition, Madonna strolled over to the judges' table and announced with her typical defiance, "I'm auditioning for this scholarship so I can work with Pearl Lang. I saw one of her performances and she's the only one I want to work with." (The recollection of this moment comes from Pearl Lang.) "Of course," Ms. Lang chortles when completing the tale, "Madonna's eyes almost came out of her head when I told her I **was** Pearl Lang." Madonna did impress the judges and was, in fact, one of six dancers in the country chosen for a scholarship to Alvin Ailey's New York studio.

Working with Pearl Lang is no small commitment. Ms. Lang is one of the grandes dames of dance, an extraordinary talent who was the lead soloist of the famed Martha Graham Dancers, one of America's most acclaimed dance troupes. Now, the artistic director for Alvin Ailey, Lang says of Madonna that "She was an exceptional dancer. Many dancers can kick and exhibit acrobatic body control, but that is just run of the mill, taken for granted.

Madonna had the power, the intensity to go beyond mere physical performance into something far more exciting. That intensity is the first thing I look for in a dancer, and Madonna had it. I was sad that she left dance, but I knew that she had the power, that she would succeed at whatever she tried. Madonna simply has the magical quality that a great artist needs."

Madonna has recalled her two years with Pearl Lang as "interesting work. The style is very archaic, angular, and dramatic. Painful, dark, and guilt-ridden: very Catholic." Many dancers consider Lang's style the most disciplined and challenging of all the major modern dance choreographers. With her eyes on success and her scholarship as an open door, Madonna took a giant step forward in her first stab at stardom. "Dance means freedom," Madonna has replied in response to a question about why dance was her first love. "Moving your body to music is the ultimate release."

The business of her dance scholarship safely secured, the

nineteen-year-old Madonna turned her attention to an arena most would consider more vital: survival. Earning enough money to pay for basic food and shelter is an unenviable task for any teenager trying to go to school in a big American city. And New York is not the cheapest or easiest city in which to live. Madonna settled her income and her housing problems by landing a job at the Dunkin' Donuts across the street from Bloomingdale's and finding herself a room in one of those areas of New York that fully explains that city's reputation as a concrete jungle.

It was not what one could view as "Fifth Avenue style," but it was a start. Of course, giving up a full scholarship at the University of Michigan to plant oneself in a tiny rat-hole room in a New York slum is a wisdom that goes wasted on most parents. "When my father came to visit," Madonna has said, "he was mortified. The place was crawling with cockroaches. There were winos in the hallways, and the entire place smelled like stale beer."

Welcome to New York!!!

2.

l get it

As 1978 rolled into 1979, Madonna found herself a wiser, if not richer, young New Yorker. She would no longer imagine that Times Square was the center of the universe, nor would she be overwhelmed by the stars of the dance world. In a town noted for its lightning pace, the little girl from Detroit learned fast. She could now see to the end of the dance world tunnel, and the sunlight—or starlight—there simply wasn't bright enough for her to endure the long dark passage.

Pearl Lang's company was well respected, but Madonna's position as one of the thirteen company members ceased to hold enough fascination for her to stay any longer. Madonna also realized that if she were to make the jump to a dance company that toured internationally, she would probably have to wait at least five years for the right position to open. Financially successful dance troupes, similarly to rock bands, are rarely open to accepting new

OVER

Dan Gilroy

members; most positions only open up because of injury, death, or retirement.

Not one to wait in line, certainly not for five years, Madonna began exploring the alternative careers that New York might offer to a beautiful young girl with a lot of talent and an open mind. Like most dancers, she traveled in very artsy circles, so her friends included many up-and-coming actors, painters, and musicians. "I used to go out with graffiti artists," she has said, not adding that she went through them like spray-paint cans. "I got in the habit of carrying markers and writing my name everywhere."

During her graffiti phase, one of Madonna's less short-lived boyfriends was Norris Burroughs, the king of graffiti T-shirt designers. Norris, who is a cross between Burt Reynolds and Batman, had a three-month relationship with Madonna that ran the gamut from friendship to dating to living together. Eventually, Burroughs, his superhero image intact, found a new girlfriend, and Madonna, never a candidate for the Lonely Hearts Club, was on the move again.

"I used to go out with graffiti artists. I got in the habit of carrying markers and writing my name everywhere."

It was at a party thrown by Norris that Madonna met Dan Gilroy, the singer/guitarist who would ultimately give Madonna the basic musical knowledge she needed to begin her move to the next plateau. Gilroy, a multi-talented painter/writer/musician, understood Madonna's artistic desire to explore new media and gave her free run of his rehearsal studio in Queens. Eventually, which is to say in a few days, Gilroy and Madonna became boyfriend and girlfriend, and much later—a few weeks—Madonna moved into Dan's studio.

Strangely enough, Norris Burroughs had actually set up the romance between his close friend Dan Gilroy and Madonna, who had recently become his ex-girlfriend. For several days before his party, Burroughs pumped up both sides with the praises of each other. Even more strangely, Gilroy was not entirely enamored of sexy Ms. Ciccone upon first glance. "At the party she was wearing these clothes that looked like a clown outfit," Gilroy recalls matter-of-factly. "She didn't make a huge impression on me at first because she seemed sort of draggy, like depressed or something." The tide turned quickly, however, as

Madonna showed Gilroy her good/sexy side, capping the evening by approaching him directly and asking "Aren't you going to kiss me?"

Dan Gilroy and his brother Ed were doing a two-man comedy act titled "The Bil and Gil Show" at the time. Dan broke the news of Madonna's moving into their studio space (a converted synagogue) to his brother, and the next thing Dan Gilroy and

Madonna capped the evening by approaching Gilroy directly and asking "Aren't you going to kiss me?"

Madonna knew, fun was everywhere: picnics, movies, concerts—fun! "I never liked heavy relationships," shrugs Gilroy, "so my scene with Madonna was great. She was going to leave for France, and we had a blast for about a month. There's something very magical about a nonbinding relationship because you know it isn't meant to last, so you can make each moment as intense as you want. It is like being on a roller coaster: you go on for a few thrills, then it is over."

Despite Madonna's newfound interest in music, there was little perception of change from her mentors in the dance world. "She had taken up singing," Pearl Lang says of Madonna's early transition to music, "but I never took much notice of it. I believe that at that time (1979), even she was unaware of how far she would take it." Indeed, at that time it would have been an unlikely prediction that Madonna's fledgling interest in music would ever evolve to the point that it has.

Although she maintained her ties to the dance world, Madonna was actively looking for bigger and better things by early 1980. She began going to movie and theatrical

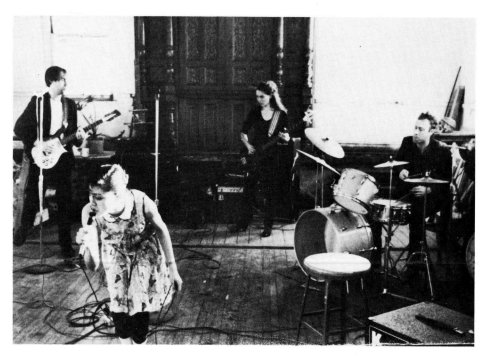

The original Breakfast Club, with Ed Gilroy on guitar (left), Angie Smit on bass (center), Dan Gilroy on drums, and Madonna on lead vocals.

auditions, landing a major spot in the Patrick Hernandez Revue, a multimedia rock/vaudeville show which took her straight to the top of European entertainment circles faster than you can say "Lucky Star."

Two big Parisian producers, Jean Claude Pellerin and Jean Van Lieu ("they both weighed 300 pounds or more," laughs Dan Gilroy), fell in love with Madonna's act and wanted to make her the biggest female star in Europe. The two Frenchmen jointly produced several TV shows in Paris and had the top-drawer French connections that could take Madonna straight to the top. The portly Parisians had just stumbled into international success with a disco hit by Hernandez, "Born to Be Alive." In fact, the French connection was in America searching for good-looking boys and girls to back Hernandez on stage for a world tour. The idea was to hide Patrick's clumsiness with a sort of New Wave a la Las Vegas revue gyrating all around him. Money was no object, since "Born to Be Alive" had grossed over $25 million worldwide.

The Hernandez people had gone to America looking for a few girls to teach the can-can to, but they left with something more than they bargained for in Madonna. At one point they were even ignoring the star they came to find backup dancers for in favor of structuring an act around little Ms. Ciccone. They even wrote a song for her titled

A rare photograph of Madonna playing drums, the first musical instrument she learned.

"She's a Real Disco Queen." They made sure Madonna had the full star treatment: a vocal coach, a dance teacher, an expensive apartment in the best part of town, a chauffeur-driven limousine, the best clothes—everything money could buy.

"Living in Paris," Madonna has said, "was like a French movie." After a few weeks, the movie started changing its plot with the speed of the Concorde. Madonna realized that her producers were taking her around Paris "to show their friends what they had found in the gutters of New York." Yes, the Frenchmen had millions of dollars, but they also had someone on their hands that money can't buy: Madonna Ciccone.

The Hernandez contingent took Madonna to all the right places in Paris, from chic restaurants and clubs to all the happening parties. They introduced Madonna to sun-tanned hip and rich French boys—whom she treated as dirt. The Frenchmen didn't realize what kind of star they were playing with. Yes, Parisian aristocrats were a far cry from the rock & rollin' American kids Madonna grew up with in Detroit and New York; there can be little doubt that her French producers thought they had won her over. Wrong. "I demanded money," Madonna recalls. "When they gave it to me, I'd run out and go riding on motor bikes with these low-life Vietnamese boys."

Always true to herself, Madonna thus made sure her Paris experience would be short-lived. The Parisians had seen in Madonna a

free. I told them that I was going home to visit. I left everything I had there and never returned."

It was not a move anyone could have anticipated. On the outside, it seemed as if Madonna had everything: money, cars, clothes, and people to serve her every whim. Who would imagine that she would return to an American slum and leave European splendor behind? Certainly not the Hernandez troupe. And certainly not Dan Gilroy, who found himself right back on the roller coaster with Madonna after an interlude of a few months. When she returned from Paris, there was one major change in Madonna: Her interest in dance had fully given way to dreams of rock superstardom.

"I had this theory," says Gilroy of those times, "that anyone with a sense of timing could be a drummer. So when Madonna came back with the music bug, I began teaching her how to play drums." Gilroy found his brother Ed a ready recruit for duties on rhythm guitar, and Madonna rounded out the group with a dancer friend of hers, Angie Smit,

Madonna realized that her producers were taking her around Paris "to show their friends what they had found in the gutters of New York."

star. But her star was not to rise over the Eiffel Tower, and certainly not as a supporting role to Patrick Hernandez. Madonna told her producers that she was homesick and talked them into letting her go back to America for a week. "It was a great adventure," Madonna has said of her time in Paris, "but I tired of it. All I wanted to do was make trouble because they stuck me in an environment that didn't let me be

who picked up bass guitar.

"Madonna was a maniac for rehearsing," remembers Gilroy. "Rehearse, rehearse, rehearse—she's a real workaholic. We'd rehearse all night and into the morning, then we'd all go out for breakfast." On the strength of multiple stacks of buckwheats at International House of Pancakes, Madonna's first band found its name: "Breakfast Club."

At this point Madonna had moved

Vintage portrait of Angie Smit, Ed Gilroy, Madonna, and Dan Gilroy

back into Gilroy's loft space in Corona, Queens. They shared what Gilroy calls "good times that came from a mishmash of fun, music, friendship, and romance." Madonna had the run of all the musical instruments in the loft while Dan and brother Ed were off to their respective jobs. Practicing ceaselessly, Madonna quickly turned her fledgling interest in music into a working knowledge of drums, guitar, and keyboards. The whole picture, filled with love, art, and song, took on the nuances of a romantic novel. "It was one of the happiest times of my life," Madonna has recalled. "I really felt loved. Sometimes I'd write some sad songs and he'd sit there and cry. Very sweet."

After several months of rehearsing, Breakfast Club, with Madonna on drums, began playing the New York club circuit—"all the Lower East Side hellholes," as Madonna has put it.

Stephen Jon Lewicki

MADONNA IN

A CERTAIN SACRIFICE

A Certain Sacrifice is a 60-minute cult thriller that features Madonna at the crux of a revenge/murder plot.

From the first, Breakfast Club had big problems, most of them generated by bass player Angie Smit. "For one," Dan Gilroy recalls, "Angie would hardly play any music live. After all our rehearsals, her performance consisted mainly of standing there staring at the audience. **Occasionally,** she might play a note or two." Compounding Smit's stance was her costume, which has been described as "several strings of beads loosely sewed together" and "something like a chain-link fence." The effect left male audience members gawking at Smit's appealing dancer's body, leaving little room for any attention to the songs themselves. "People looked at us," concludes Gilroy, "like a strip show."

Madonna and the other members of Breakfast Club eventually convinced Angie to pursue other endeavors and leave the band. The next move was a touch more bold: Barely six months into her musical career, Madonna began her charge for the spotlight and convinced Dan Gilroy to write two songs for her. At first it made Breakfast Club an interesting avant garde act: Madonna would play drums for a few songs, then come out from behind the skins, grab the mike, and belt out her two numbers. For a while it all seemed to click, but eventually Breakfast Club began looking like two acts competing for the same stage. "I was just a lot more goal-oriented and commercial than they were," Madonna has assessed the Breakfast Club times. "I took advantage of the situation because I knew I could make it work to my benefit."

By early 1980, Madonna left Breakfast Club and started her own band, planting herself firmly behind the microphone from the start. The

band went for the classic rock rehearsal space, a garage in Queens, and ran through names faster than an escaped convict. The band eventually settled on the name Emmenon, which Madonna later modified to Emmy. Her bass player at this time was Gary Burke (who, coincidentally, joined the revived version of Breakfast Club in 1983).

When drummer Mike Monahan got married and left Emmy, Madonna got a call that must have seemed from the heavens: It was from Steve Bray, the waiter she had met back at college, and he wanted to move—with his drums—to New York. "I found that, oddly enough, she needed a drummer," reflected Bray. "So I said, 'Fine, I'll be there next week.' "

With the wheels of music spinning in her head, the charms of the dance world were now thin to Madonna. For her, the whole scene at the Alvin Ailey Dance Workshop started looking like some half-baked version of **Fame**. "Let me tell you," Madonna has reflected matter-of-factly. "My experience has nothing at all to do with that particular brand of escapism—only a sucker would believe that stuff!" Her commitment to modern dance, like that to Breakfast Club, was about to go the way of all flesh.

A third force, added to dance and music, became a strong element in Madonna's career by this time: acting. Responding to a trade newspaper ad announcing auditions for a starring role in an avant garde film, Madonna caught the eye of writer/director Stephen Jon Lewicki. Madonna's approach to securing her audition was a novel one: a two-page, handwritten letter accompanied by an assortment of snapshots. It stood out from the lot of your prototypical "real" actress

materials that Lewicki had received, all of which contained the standard, neatly-typed resume and an ultra-professional head-shot photograph.

"Her approach was strange," reflects Lewicki, "very strange, but I decided to follow up on it." Lewicki called up Madonna and arranged to meet her in Washington Square Park, which is Lewicki's own method of audition. A brilliant man who majored in philosophy at Columbia University, Lewicki has a unique and highly personal approach to film, necessitating his unusual method for auditions, the personal conversation. What Lewicki found in Madonna was a ravishing woman/child with an intensity to match his own. "From the moment I met her," Lewicki recalls, "I knew she was a star. She fit the role perfectly and had a riveting personality. She has the charisma that makes a star a star." He hired her almost immediately, over nearly 100 applicants, and Madonna became the only featured member of the cast who was chosen as a result of an audition—the others all having been referred to Lewicki by producers, writers, and actors he knew.

"Madonna is a very complex individual," Lewicki assesses. "As an actress she is the consummate professional: on time, understands her role, always delivers her lines. But she has an incredible swing of moods in her personal life. She can express deep love then fiery hatred for the same thing—or person— within a few minutes' time." Lewicki is not the only one to notice Madonna's roller-coaster approach to emotional stability. "I'm very indecisive," Madonna has said of herself, "Yes—no—yes. In my career I make pretty good decisions, but in my personal life I make constant havoc by

◀ Madonna hangs from her heels in this promotional photo for **A Certain Sacrifice.**

changing my mind every five minutes."

Madonna's role in Lewicki's film, **A Certain Sacrifice**, required the use of many complex thoughts and emotions. In it she played the part of Bruna, a bad girl living in post-punk New York who falls in love with an equally bad boy named Dashiel. The two leading roles, to give you an idea, were tailor made for Nastassja Kinski and Sean Penn. In the movie, Bruna (Madonna) gets raped by an older man whom she and her boyfriend then track down and kill. Although **Independent Film & Video Monthly** called it "a bizarre story of urban terror, the film has humorous touches as well.

Although **A Certain Sacrifice** didn't make Madonna rich (she earned exactly $100) or famous (the 60-minute video cassette is just beginning to be available as of February 1985), she did get one very valuable thing out of it: acting experience in front of a camera. In view of her tremendous performance right at the beginning of her rock video career, one would have to assume that the endless hours of work Madonna put into **A Certain Sacrifice** paid off handsomely. The movie now, some five years after Madonna acted in it, yields valuable insights into the intensity of one of the world's hottest stars. Yes, her character is spotty in places but the overview of her performance as bad girl Bruna can only leave the viewer with the pleasant knowledge that he is seeing the seminal work of an important artist. File the film in the drawer marked "cult classic."

Like a juggler, Madonna managed to keep her three careers—music, dance, and acting—in constant motion. But by mid-1980 even the faintest desire to continue in pursuit

Breakfast Club ultimately broke up because it began to look like two acts at once: one fronted by Madonna, the other by Dan Gilroy, who now leads a reborn, 1985 version of Breakfast Club.

of modern dance superstardom had dimmed to the level of a power failure. Seven days a week of dance classes couldn't fit Madonna's busy schedule, and no one around her at this time had the perception of her as a dancer by any purist standards. Over the course of about eight months—beginning from the time Dan Gilroy began teaching her drums—Madonna had completely changed directions, transforming herself from a dancer to a singer. Visions of pointe shoes and leotards gathered dust in her memory. She was a rock star now.

When Steve Bray finally made it to New York, complete with his drum kit, Madonna's stock in her own rock & roll future went up considerably. "He was a lifesaver," Madonna has recalled. "I wasn't a good enough company jugular—which is to say, its checkbook.

With Bray on the drums, Madonna as guitarist/vocalist, and various members shuffling through the other instruments, her band, Emmy, set out to make its mark. She played several financially unsuccessful concerts at an odd collection of some of New York's worst clubs, all of which served to dampen the spirits of her band. In New York, musicians stay loyal only to that which makes them a living, so, with the exception of Bray, her band put on walking shoes once it became apparent that the big bucks weren't falling out of the sky. Madonna was a new face on the music scene, and Bray was even newer, but the word was already out that her bands weren't making money. In a town full of musical

"I'm very indecisive: yes—no—yes. In my career I make pretty good decisions, but in my personal life I make constant havoc by changing my mind every five minutes."

musician to be screaming at anybody about how badly they were playing." With Bray by her side—and in her arms, for that matter—Madonna felt a sense of musical potential that was more real than ever before. She was no longer worried about booking her band into rat-hole New York clubs for $25; it was a big-time record deal she was after. Writing and recording music in Bray's little home studio, Madonna began to smell blood down the musical trail and, no doubt, had all the confidence to go for the record mercenaries, this was a big drawback.

The situation was far from idyllic for Madonna in 1980. She'd given up her dance scholarship—and her dance career, for that matter—and found herself at age 20 with no money, no home to speak of, few friends, and no band. But Madonna is a survivor, a girl who thinks about results, not the odds against her. She needed money, a band, a rehearsal space, a recording studio, and time to get it together. What it all boiled down to was that Madonna desperately needed one thing: a miracle.

T here is an exceedingly ugly and decaying old shack of a high rise hovering above one of New York's worst neighborhoods in which hundreds of rock bands live, rehearse, and record. Its name: the Music Building. In late 1980, down but not out, Madonna was there looking to rent a rehearsal space when she shot a corny line to a guy who had just come off the elevator. "Hey," she joked, "you look like John Lennon." The man's name was Adam Alter and—as things tend to go in Madonna's storybook life—he owned a music rehearsal studio and a rock & roll management company, knew a lot of musicians, and, conveniently, had money.

Alter, as most men do, fell for Madonna hook, line, and sinker. "I had just formed Gotham Productions," recalls Alter of his first close encounter of the Madonna kind, "so my partner and I were looking for acts to manage and

LUCKY
STAR

Adam Alter

produce. It was," he shrugs in a puff of smoke, "good timing."

After listening to Madonna's demo tape, Alter introduced Madonna to his partner, Camille Barbone, who only confirmed his initial assessment of Madonna's star potential. "Right from the first," Alter states without qualification, "Camille and I were certain that Madonna was destined for great things. We wanted her to become a rock/pop multimedia superstar appealing to everyone from little kids to adult theatre goers. To say we believed in her is an understatement. We signed her immediately."

With the business of miracle hunting temporarily put to rest, Madonna put her two feet back on the ground. She was now signed to Gotham Management, which opened up a whole new horizon for her. The Gotham Studio was used regularly by Melba Moore, Johnny Winter, and David Johansen, among others, all of whom the 20-year-old Madonna got to know.

Madonna's contract with Gotham Management was nothing like the megabucks rock contracts that make the news in **Rolling Stone.** Nonetheless, she managed to move out of the rooming house she lived in

"We wanted her to become a rock/pop multimedia superstar. . . . To say that we believed in her is an understatement. We signed her immediately."

("a place filled with prostitutes, degenerates, and escaped convicts," recalls Adam Alter) to a share in a decent Upper West Side apartment. It was not Hollywood glory, but it was safe. The set-up, for the time, looked pretty good: an apartment and a rehearsal space, both paid for by Gotham Management, a salary (reports vary, but it seems to have been $100 a week), and a catalog of musicians to choose from for her new band, all of whom would be paid by Gotham.

The entire negotiation went smoothly, Madonna's only real demand being that Steve Bray remain her drummer. "Camille was against that," remembers Adam Alter, "but Gotham—Camille and I—eventually agreed to it because we knew it would make Madonna happy."

As in Paris, Madonna's management generally bent over backwards to accommodate her whims. The big difference between

One of the first studio photographs of Madonna as a blonde.

the Parisians and Gotham, other than geography, was that the New York-based company was operating on far less capital. Still, Madonna felt at home, and by late 1980, things really were looking good.

Like the Parisians, however, Gotham made a few tragic mistakes in dealing with Madonna. For one, Alter and Barbone tried to steer her away from the music she likes because they thought it wasn't commercial. They envisioned her as a clean-cut, somewhat sophisticated Sheena Easton type, an image diametrically opposed to what Madonna loved—streetwise downtown funk. "They (Gotham) weren't used to that stuff," the child of Motown has recalled, "and I'd agreed to do rock & roll. But my heart wasn't into it."

Following her reason rather than her heart has always been a tough act for Madonna. More often than not, the passionate side wins out. "That's the Latin in me," Ms. Ciccone has assessed.

As she had done at Gilroy's studio in Queens, Madonna was working around the clock in Gotham's rehearsal studio as soon as she was given the green light to use the studio free of charge. "We tried to get her TV commercials and movie deals," recalls Alter of those 1980

"Madonna is very emotional," Alter explains. "When she's sad or in a bad mood, she can't do anything. But get her in the right circumstances and she'll set the studio on fire with hits."

John Sex started getting hot on the New York nightclub circuit around the same time as Madonna and Brian (Stray Cats) Setzer.

days in the Music Building, "but she didn't want to be bothered. At that time all she did was stay in the studio all day and write songs. She was turned off by any vision of herself except being a rock star. It's funny," laughs Alter, "that now she's doing all the things we wanted her to do four years ago."

By 1981 Madonna had a small cult following, and the buzz was out that New York had three new stars: a cute blond boy named Brian Setzer in a weird band called the Bloodless Pharaohs; a wild multimedia act fronted by actor/singer/stripper John Sex; and, of course, the then raven-haired Latin, Madonna. Setzer went on to form the Stray Cats, and John Sex, who appears in a recent Cars video fondling his pet boa constrictor, has been signed to Island records. Setzer, Sex, and Madonna are some trio by any standard.

Madonna and Steve Bray worked ceaselessly, writing rock songs by day and scouring the rock clubs at night for any leads they could find. Gotham managed to book Madonna's band, still using the name Emmy, into a chain of clubs with unlikely names such as Chase Park, Botany Talk House, and My Father's Place. Bray has remembered Emmy's earlier music as "really raucous rock & roll influenced by the Pretenders and the Police," but by 1981 Madonna's music had been toned down, and she was writing and singing some beautiful ballads to round out her rock repertoire.

"Madonna, like most good artists," Adam Alter explains, "is very emotional. When she's sad or in a bad mood, she can't do anything. But get her in the right circumstances and she'll set the studio on fire with hits. That girl can write, sing, and perform hits."

Two open wounds, which never healed, began to strain the relationship between Madonna and Gotham Management. The first, predictably, involved money and expectations. Alter, and especially Camille Barbone, had pumped Madonna's head full of big dreams. Invariably, Barbone would unfurl a long list of superlatives when introducing Madonna to anyone, praise and predictions that were both heartfelt and well intended (as well as, ultimately, accurate). Madonna was being silver-spooned pure stardust, but in time she began to wonder where the gold dust was. "Sometimes, I blame myself, Camille blames herself," states Alter flatly. "Madonna was a very modest, humble girl when we met her, and the two of us treated her like a star before she was a star. Camille especially inflated her head with the star thing in a way that, in retrospect, was unbelievable."

But as Madonna's lucky star slowly rose, the money in the Gotham till was draining fast. After nearly a year with Gotham she found herself, with the exception of having recorded four songs which could potentially be sold, with little more than she began with. There were many promises of record deals, indeed some very substantial promises, but for a young girl riding in the fast lane, promises don't pay for the dry cleaning. The pressure was on Gotham Management to make money fast, and the buzz in the air said that if Madonna's tape wasn't sold right away there would be trouble in Gotham City.

"It all became like a race," summarizes Alter, "the big race to get the big money by selling the tape. We had the star, we had the

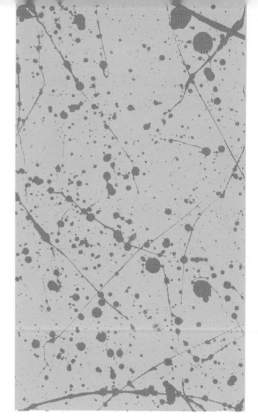

songs, and everything was right. The only problem was there were too many egos clashing around. Everyone wanted a piece of Madonna." The egos fought a psychological business war that surrounded Madonna on all fronts: Booking agents wanted their piece, and talent scouts from major companies like William Morris made promises and demands. But the bottom line was that Gotham couldn't get anyone to put it all down on paper. The first open wound—money—could no longer be hidden, and things looked bad for Gotham. "There were days," Alter recalls somberly, "that I would go to the bank and there was nothing there. N-O-T-H-I-N-G. It had all been spent promoting Madonna."

Yet Madonna too had nothing—she didn't even own the tape with four cuts that she recorded and Gotham Management had helped produce. The "Gotham Tape," as it has come to be known, has four songs on it: "I Want You," which was actually written for Camille Barone, "Society's Boy," "Love on the Run," and "Get Up." All four tunes are potential hits but, unfortunately, hits that remain to this day in limbo, in a complicated entanglement of legal red tape entwining a veritable army of potential owners.

("I suspect that nothing will ever happen with those early tapes," Alter reflects a bit sadly, "because the music industry overproduces so much that any tune with the slightest complication generally never makes it to radio land. Thousands of great tunes never get heard. It's sad, but true, that an artist like John Lennon had to die before we got to hear his early songs.")

By early 1982 any pretense of a tight bond between Madonna and Gotham became gossamer-thin. Madonna was more than familiar with the New York music scene at this point, and she was a hot face on the club circuit. She worked on her ballads and rock tunes for Gotham by day, but her nights were rarely spent haunting the clubs her rock/ballad material was being made for. Instead she and Steve Bray went in for downtown funkiness, dancing the night away in discos like Danceteria, Paradise Garage, and the Roxy.

As Gotham's money ran out, and the band with the money, Madonna studied her situation carefully and decided that there was something wrong with the whole picture, something even money couldn't cure. It became evident to Madonna that she really didn't like her own songs and that she was being pushed into becoming something she wasn't. "I wanted to do more funky stuff," Madonna has recalled. "Finally I said, 'Forget it, I can't do this anymore. I'm going to have to start

all over.' " Open wound number two was lack of artistic freedom; prognosis: fatal.

The breakup of Madonna and Gotham was about as amicable as the French and German dispute over the Alsace-Lorraine. Both sides had their allies and, as in any war, accusations flew. But neither Madonna nor Alter is the type of character that stands around screaming uselessly for long, and the two picked up their respective

scene. "I was spinning records at Danceteria," Kamins remembers, "and Madonna was tearing up the dance floor. She came up to the DJ booth and introduced herself, then we started going out to clubs together." Thus Kamins joined the conga line of men who fell for the Motown Siren. "I was flirting with him," Madonna has coyly admitted of her first excursion into Kamin's booth.

When Kamins met Madonna he

"Everyone wanted a piece of Madonna." The egos fought a psychological business war that surrounded Madonna on all fronts.

marbles and headed for new games in new circles.

(As of 1985, Alter is producing a musical about his father, who was a legendary character in vaudeville. Part of the financing for Alter's production comes, circuitously, from Madonna. In view of the fact that Madonna, according to Alter, "never dissolved her contract with Gotham Management in the proper, legal fashion," Gotham sued her for, and won, payment for all the "free" studio time and rehearsals Madonna had at Gotham's expense. The settlement, according to Alter, was small.

As for the infamous "Gotham Tape," it remains locked up in a complicated legal battle. The inside track, however, belongs neither to Gotham nor Madonna. The tape is in possession of Media Sound, the studio that Gotham hired to record Madonna's four songs, and Media seems to have the best legal position in the matter.)

It was time for a miracle again and, true to her name, Madonna found one fast. This one arrived in the shape of Mark Kamins, a young record producer who was also the hottest DJ on the New Wave club

Mark Kamins had his eye on Madonna and his ear to the radio.

had just finished producing an album for Capitol Records, a deal he got by writing a novelty song called "Snapshot." "I was looking for more record deals," Kamins relates, "something else to produce in the studio. I've always been the DJ type—the kid who plays records at parties—and the moment I got into a recording studio I knew I wanted to

be a producer."

Madonna gave Kamins a tape she had made with Steve Bray on a little home-level tape recorder. It contained four songs: "Burning Up," "Everybody," "Stay," and "Ain't No Big Deal." Kamins loved it and immediately contacted Michael Rosenblatt, a rising young executive at Warner Brothers' Sire Records. Kamins had met Rosenblatt when Kamins produced a dance record with David Byrne, whose band Talking Heads is on Sire Records. Even more importantly, Kamins understood that Rosenblatt, along with another young executive named Michael Alago, was at the heart of Warner Brothers' famed "Kiddie Corps," the new wave of young talent scouts who had their ears to the radio, their eyes on the nightclubs, and their hearts set on discovering the best young musical artists in the business.

Furthermore, Kamins was a dance-mix master producer, and Madonna was a dance-oriented act. That made it even more natural to take the tape to Rosenblatt, who had earned his talent scout spurs by recommending the B-52s, a white dance act, to Sire in 1977, when the industry buzzword was "punk."

"Mark Kamins had told me that there was this incredibly attractive female singer that I should meet," recalls Rosenblatt, "so I took him up on his offer to introduce me to her. I was out on the town with the guys from Wham when all of our heads got turned around by this incredibly wild-looking, beautiful girl who was on her way up to the DJ booth. I immediately knew it was Madonna, introduced myself, and said, "When you have your tape ready, I'd love to hear it."

About a week later Kamins and

The rock dream lives on: Superscout Michael Rosenblatt signed Madonna less than an hour after hearing her demo tape—and still combs the clubs for new talent.

There was one slight catch. Seymour Stein, notorious genius, wild man, and president of Sire Records, was in the hospital, and no deal with Sire Records can be finalized without Seymour's written approval. Rosenblatt played Madonna's tape for Stein at the hospital that very afternoon. Stein loved it and set up a meeting of the four of them— Rosenblatt, Kamins, Madonna, and himself—for the next day.

Needless to say, the experience of meeting, playing her tape for, and completing a contract negotiation with Stein in his hospital room is a detail of Madonna's life that remains quite alive in her memory. "Here I am going into a hospital," she has recalled fondly, "to meet this man I've never met before who's sitting there in his jockey shorts with a drip feed in his arm!"

Regardless of the influence of any hospital-induced drugging, Stein's judgment was sound on Madonna. Stein, who also signed the Talking Heads and the Pretenders, among others, added another smart find to his reputation as a freewheeling man of great vision. It wasn't a huge record contract, nothing like the six- and seven-figure deals that Madonna gets now, but it was a real contract for real money.

The whole thing happened so quickly that it resembles a Hollywood B movie plot. Madonna seems to be a magnet for miracles and has assessed the entire picture with typical nonchalance. Despite all the clauses in the contract about publishing, litigation, alteration, accounting, royalties, and world rights, Madonna reduced all the record deal negotiating to a single question in her mind: "What did I have to lose?"

She signed on the dotted line.

Madonna showed up at Rosenblatt's office with the tape. "I listened to the four cuts on the tape, then I rolled it back and listened to the first song again," recalls Rosenblatt vividly. "That was enough for me." When Rosenblatt asked Madonna what she wanted to do, she had two words for him: "Make records." Equally as directly, Rosenblatt countered, "Let's go!"

Before Madonna left his office, Rosenblatt had drawn up a preliminary contract on a yellow scratch pad outlining costs, advance money, and production dollars. In slightly more than one hour from turning on the tape recorder, Kamins, Madonna, and Rosenblatt had agreed in principle to a record deal. This, friends, is a **real** miracle.

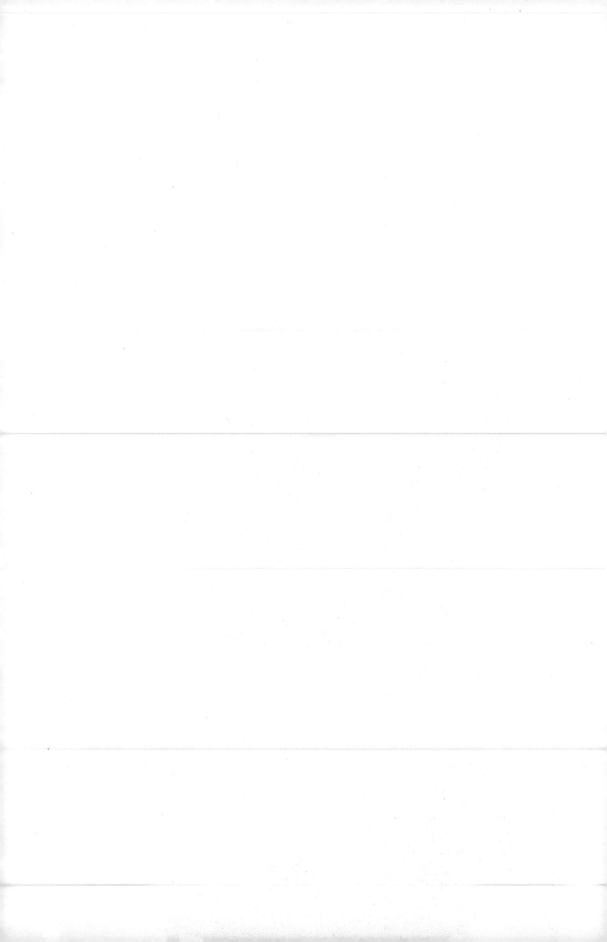

4.

oVER

BorDer

tHE

N

ow the fun began. After four years of beating her head against the wall to make the scene in New York, Madonna, not yet 23 years old, had a cast on her side that could satisfy her fiery competitive spirit. All at once she was working with a megabucks international record company, Sire/Warner Brothers; two top executives who would fend for her, Seymour Stein and Michael Rosenblatt; and a producer who was one of her best friends, Mark Kamins. For some the world turns; for others it spins like a top.

liNE

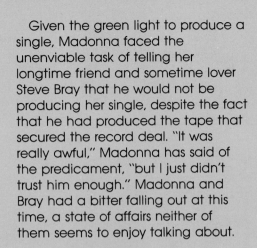

Given the green light to produce a single, Madonna faced the unenviable task of telling her longtime friend and sometime lover Steve Bray that he would not be producing her single, despite the fact that he had produced the tape that secured the record deal. "It was really awful," Madonna has said of the predicament, "but I just didn't trust him enough." Madonna and Bray had a bitter falling out at this time, a state of affairs neither of them seems to enjoy talking about.

"Music is a business, and I spend a fortune, literally, trying to break an act. It is imperative that the artist respect that investment," says Michael Rosenblatt.

(Fortunately, the quarrel has been resolved since then, and the duo has resumed collaborating on hit songs.)

The producer's chair for Madonna's first single went to the man who put her record deal together, Mark Kamins. Kamins chose the instruments, hired the musicians and the engineer, rented the studio, and oversaw all aspects of musical production. But it was Rosenblatt who made the critical decision of which tunes would comprise Madonna's first single: "Everybody," was selected as the B side, and "Ain't No Big Deal," the song that was ultimately responsible for landing the record deal, was picked to be her first single.

Whatever Madonna's opinion was about which songs should go out first is anyone's guess. Yes, she had a past history of playing the spoiled star with people, but when the big money was on the table she played it as has proven to be her style: as a team player and true professional. "Madonna," summarizes Michael Rosenblatt of his experience in

Madonna in Hell's Kitchen

breaking her into the world of the big-time, "is great. She will do anything to be a star, and that's exactly what I look for in an artist: **total** cooperation. I want that artist to be there to do whatever I need. Music is a business, after all, and I—my company—spend a fortune, literally, trying to break an act. It is imperative that the artist respect that investment. I try not to deal with artists who think 'Music is fun: I can meet people, travel, and get laid a lot.'

"With Madonna, I knew I had someone hot and cooperative, so I planned to build her career with singles, rather than just put an album out right away and run the risk of disaster. Madonna is a unique talent in that she can sing, dance, and act, and she looks fabulous. Therefore I was able to do unique planning with her career, and it was incredibly satisfying to see all the pieces fall into place."

From the start, Madonna was treated with great respect by Warner Brothers. Remember, this is the record company that sticks its label on

Prince, Van Halen, and the Pretenders, among others, so it doesn't often roll out the red carpet for rookie rock stars. But then again, Madonna was no ordinary rookie.

Rosenblatt had goosed the Warner Brothers publicity department enough to get a tentative yes for a promotional budget for the now bleached-blond beauty. As a matter of company policy, no Warner Brothers artist ever gets publicity on the release of a single unless it is part of an album. If rules were made to be broken, clearly Madonna is among those who rules were made to be broken for.

Rosenblatt and Warner Brothers waited breathlessly for Madonna, Kamins, and crew to finish up the two cuts in the studio. In less than three weeks, Kamins, Madonna, and Rosenblatt huddled in the studio, ears tuned to what was intended to be Madonna's first release, "Ain't No Big Deal." True to its title, unfortunately, Rosenblatt nixed the tune, feeling that it had lost its original vitality and lacked a commercial edge. All was not lost,

The world premiere of Madonna's act was at Danceteria as part of trendsetter Haoui Montaug's No Entiendes Cabaret.

The King of Cabaret, Haoui Montaug.

however, for when the B side tune was played, everything that wasn't riveted to the floor bounced to the music. "The moment I heard 'Everybody,' I knew that Madonna was off to a great start," says Rosenblatt.

There was enthusiasm but also some tension because "Ain't No Big Deal" was a mistake. Warner Brothers had sent Madonna into the studio to make two cuts, but only one song was usable. "It forced me," Rosenblatt recalls, "to put 'Everybody' on both sides of the single." But this kind of mistake is like accidentally buying a lottery ticket when you wanted a train ticket and then winning the million-dollar jackpot, for "Everybody" launched Madonna like a nuclear rocket; virtually every dance-oriented radio station in the country picked up on it, and the song raced up to the Top Ten on the dance charts like a thoroughbred. So much for mistakes.

Madonna put together a little act to showcase her new single and, appropriately, the location of her world premiere for her modest four-person revue was Danceteria, the club where producer Mark Kamins had long been the DJ. Madonna and her three dancers—Erica, Bags, and Martin Burgoyne—appeared as part of the No Entiendes (Spanish for "You Don't Understand") Cabaret run by New York trendsetter Haoui Montaug. Montaug's cabaret had become quite a downtown tradition at this point, having produced a wide variety of acts that included everything from clowns, fire-eaters, and jugglers to exceptionally esoteric acts like the Downtown Sissies or Chi Chi Valente and the Sleazebuckets.

With Montaug decked out in a top hat and tails, suffice to say that Madonna's debut was marked by heavy brushstrokes of the wild and crazy. "She was like a disco act backed by avant garde dancers," summarizes Montaug. "I guess you could say Madonna was the first New Wave disco music."

Seated at a table right by the stage were Michael Rosenblatt, Seymour Stein, and other top-drawer execs from Sire Records. What they witnessed was a crowd of about 300 people going utterly wild over their newly signed artist. It indicated that the visual image of Madonna lip-synching with a few dancers executing simple choreography was enough to really turn people on.

Rosenblatt put two and two together: Both sides of "Everybody" were wiping up the dance charts, and both sides of Madonna—her good looks and her acting/dancing ability—were impressive as well. It added up to video, and since Madonna didn't have a band, she also immediately recognized the importance of making a tape. "I love performing on stage," Madonna has said, "but it is very taxing to go on

Video producer Ed Steinberg, who now owns the megamillion-dollar corporation Rockamerica, made her first video, "Everybody."

the road and travel in a bus. Video has made it possible to reach the masses without touring."

Like every beginning artist, the first big obstacle Madonna faced in attempting to enter the video market was an already familiar nemesis: money. Sure, Michael Jackson, the Rolling Stones, and Duran Duran could put up the big bucks—$500,000-plus in some cases—for a video, but Madonna wasn't about to get that kind of gold for her first video. But she also knew that the public doesn't care how much you spend on the video; it only cares how good the video is—period. Madonna and her team knew that the first video had to be great, even though the budget wouldn't be. She

wanted the best for almost nothing; she wanted yet another miracle.

With the wisdom of Buddha, Rosenblatt picked up the telephone, dialed, smiled, and explained his situation. As he had hoped, even expected, Rosenblatt was given the cool reply of "No problem." This response came from Ed Steinberg, the eminent video producer and founder of Rock America, the company responsible for mass distribution of rock videos to clubs. Since "Everybody" had busted loose in the clubs, Steinberg was well aware of the visuals the tune needed to climb the dance charts; Steinberg had the clubs in American logged into a computer, so he knew all the chart action of dance videos from their beginnings to their end points. In a matter of a few days, Madonna had her dancers together and Steinberg had the film crew ready.

"Madonna is incredibly cool under pressure," says Steinberg. "The day I shot 'Everybody,' one of her three backup dancers didn't show up, which would have cracked most people under the circumstances. Madonna stayed in complete control. Very patiently and very efficiently, she rechoreographed the entire song, following all of my directions for what would and wouldn't work on video. Madonna is hot on video for the simple reason that she is a class act.

"Working with Madonna is like working with Michael Jackson: She's

"Working with Madonna is like working with Michael Jackson," says Steinberg. "She's a uniquely talented performer who can dance, sing, and act incredibly well."

a uniquely talented performer who can dance, sing, and act incredibly well. She's a director's dream because all one needs to do to get a great video is to faithfully record her performance rather than, as with many acts, rely on audiovisual trickery."

Like her subsequent video for "Lucky Star," "Everybody" features Madonna's dance performance and choreography, an unusual blend of modern dance movements and streetwise rhythm. And, as with every video she has ever released, her stunning visual presence carried an already successful song to megahit proportions. "Everybody," a low-budget single with a nearly no-budget video, shot to number three on the dance charts and even cracked the top 100 pop hits despite the lack of an album to support it. As the sales of "Everybody" flashed past the 250,000 mark, Madonna's support over at Warner Brothers grew exponentially, and money for a second twelve-inch single was budgeted immediately.

While one might expect that, on the basis of the first hit, Mark Kamins would be the producer, he had to bite the bullet a la Steve Bray. Madonna and the brain trust at Warner, now that there was real cash on the line, decided that it was time to get a more experienced producer in the studio. They chose Reggie Lucas, a producer known for his work with female vocalists, and he wrote a song for Madonna after watching her perform her lip-synch and dance act at a club. Revealingly, he called the song "Physical Attraction," and it too became a huge hit on the dance charts.

At the time, Kamins, like Bray, was upset, but time seems to have

healed the hurt. "When I first met Madonna," Kamins says, recalling the spring of 1982, "she was very innocent but really ambitious. She was broke, confused, having management and personal problems; she was living a hard life. But beyond her problems I could see something special. She was a star—I could **feel** it.

"This helps me now, because I look for people with that same aura, that same vibe, and I work with them right from the beginning of their careers. I love discovering new talent," Kamins says emphatically. "That's why I think my experience working with Madonna was so valuable: I learned so much."

Kamins is now considered to be in the royal circle of dance-mix artists, having reworked "Our House" by Madness and Kajagoogoo's "Too Shy," among others. His most recent new talent project is producing the work of the inimitable John Sex.

"Physical Attraction" pushed Madonna over the borderline: with two hit singles under her "Boy Toy" belt, Warner Brothers' market research department felt confident that a Madonna album could produce substantial worldwide sales. Based on his writing ability, excellent guitar work, and the first-rate production he exhibited on "Physical Attraction," Reggie Lucas was hired to make the album with Madonna. To say it was a wise choice would be an understatement: In addition to his top-drawer work as producer, Lucas also wrote "Borderline," one of the best songs on Madonna's first album.

A curious aura surrounds the song "Ain't No Big Deal," the tune whose initial failure was responsible for the release of "Everybody." Since it was the song most responsible for getting

Madonna's initial contract, there has always been a big push to release it as a single. It was, in fact, once again planned to be the figurehead of Madonna's ship, and Reggie Lucas was given license to go full-steam ahead with it. "Unbelievably," Rosenblatt recalls with rolling eyes, "the song, yet again, didn't work out. The supposed lead song of the album was simply unusable."

The first album, whose original title was planned as **Lucky Star** with a feature play for "Ain't No Big Deal," was already over budget and now replacing the key song was a big sore spot. Thinking on his feet, Rosenblatt decided to shuffle Madonna out to L.A. and let her sweet talk the big money men in the main office personally. "She was so warm and bubbly," says Rosenblatt,

"Burning Up"

"Borderline"

"so much fun, that everybody out there loved her. This accomplished, I explained that 'Ain't No Big Deal' **had** to be replaced on the album; they gave us more money, and we went back to the studio to record another song."

The other song turned out to be "Holiday," a tune contributed by Madonna's then-boyfriend Jellybean Benitez. Madonna and Jellybean recorded "Holiday" with magical ease, producing the song from start to finish in one day. The result was inarguable: "Holiday" was the runaway choice to be the album's first single, a choice for which there will never be regrets. "Holiday" was released in June of 1983 and was a modest summer success. But when the Thanksgiving/Christmas holiday season rolled around, the song went through the roof and Madonna took a quantum leap toward becoming a household word.

Despite three hits on the dance charts and the rather healthy crossover success of "Holiday," Madonna had still not gained an inch of airplay on the mesmerizing one-eyed god of music, MTV. "We just figured we couldn't do it with 'Holiday,' " explains Rosenblatt, "because it was too dance-oriented for the MTV format. The way an artist gets airplay on MTV is when a major record company, such as Warner Brothers, goes to bat for the artist, demonstrating that they are solidly behind the act. That is what we did for 'Burning Up.' "

Madonna and MTV are a combination that is as clear and perfect as mountain water. "Burning Up," her MTV icebreaker, showcases Madonna's animal sexuality with more intensity than any of her videos to date. Written by Madonna, the song builds on a chain of sexually submissive lyrics until it reaches the untoppable "Unlike the others, I'll do anything/I'm not the same, I have no shame." Note that the rather severe blond man who drives the car in the video is a painter named Kenny Compton, who during those days in mid-1983 was another Madonna paramour.

As 1984 rolled around, Madonna's place in pop music was admirable indeed: Four singles had been released, and all four were hits, each bigger than the next. Rosenblatt's "wildest dream for the album—a couple of hundred thousand sales"— had already been achieved.

With her first album approaching gold, "Holiday" cruising at the top of the dance charts for five straight weeks, and MTV finally enraptured by "Borderline," Madonna could afford to joke about anything. "I used to worry about surviving—what I was going to eat," she has said of her days amidst poverty. "But now I have to worry about being ripped off: if my lawyer is making the right deals, if my accountant is paying me. Boring stuff like that."

The world according to Madonna.

ISLAND

MADONNA Virgin Pop
Art **ERIC FISCHL**
NEW HOLLYWOOD
Black to Black **FASHION**
POLITENESS etc

MATERIAL

GIRL

With the MTV door open, the red carpet thrown out, and millions of MTV viewers and radio listeners waiting, 1984 promised to be a good year for Madonna. "Borderline" had built a monument on the ground "Holiday" and "Burning Up" had broken, and Madonna Ciccone was a rock superstar before her twenty-fifth birthday. Her first album, **Madonna,** was so hot that the music industry buzz was out: "What can she possibly follow it up with?"

In February 1984, Madonna completed the video for her song "Lucky Star." A video officially completed less than a week after "Borderline," "Lucky Star" was not released as a single or video for several months, waiting its turn as "Borderline" climbed the industry charts. The album had already been out for nearly nine months and no one had expected a low-budget debut album by an essentially unknown artist to last this long, let alone still be growing.

It is noteworthy that Madonna's fabulous success was achieved without a band and without anything resembling a live tour. The ironic part is that live performance may well be her strongest point. Other than a few lip-synching and dancing "special guest" performances in a couple of small American and European clubs, Madonna has not had the benefit of showcasing her imposing talents live on stage.

It is impossible to know how much live performances, a world tour for instance, could have helped the sales of Madonna's first album. Because she is a solo artist, the cost of maintaining a band is phenomenally high: Paid rehearsals, salaries, costumes, hotels, meals, transportation, equipment, and a hundred other miscellaneous expenses routinely bring the cost of a world tour into the $1 million-plus range. "I think video has been very important to my success," Madonna stated flatly. "There's a lot more risk involved in live performance than video, because there are so many things that can go wrong."

Little was going wrong for Madonna by the summer of 1984. The simultaneous release of the single and video for "Lucky Star" sent the album climbing yet again. Like each single that preceded it, "Lucky Star" sold faster **and** longer than any record Madonna had previously released. "That single," observed Michael Rosenblatt, "sent album sales through the roof. I mean how many hits were on that album?" The correct answer is six, six Top Ten dance hits on a debut album: Michael Jackson territory. Of the eight songs on the first album, the only two tunes that were not released as singles are "Think of Me" and "I Know It"—both great songs as well.

As "Lucky Star" drove the LP over the 1 million mark, then doubled the platinum figure just for good measure, Madonna's only problem was boredom. She had started recording these songs on her first album as far back as mid-1982, and like any good artist, Madonna was anxious to move on to new material rather than seep in the juices of the old. But what could she do, compete against herself?

The phenomenal success of "Lucky Star" postponed the release of her second album, single, and video of the same name, **Like a Virgin.** The video for "Like a Virgin," shot on location in Venice, Italy, was completed and ready to roll by July 18, 1984. The video sat on the shelf for four months, its release postponed again and again because "Lucky Star" was holding her rock steady, high on the dance, adult contemporary, black, and rock

passionate man who lives life to the hilt." The reason she gives for the shift in producers is simply that "Nile Rodgers is a genius."

Whether Rodgers is a genius or not is open to discussion, but one point remains unarguable: The man is hot, on the money, and in the chips. Before Madonna's album, he produced **Let's Dance** for David Bowie, and soon afterward he produced the "Wild Boys" single for Duran Duran. Like Madonna, Rodgers

The video of "Like A Virgin" sat on the shelf for four months because the success of "Lucky Star" postponed the release of the new record.

charts. The postponing of an album due to the success of another is an almost unheard of event in the music world.

You would think that, in view of the first album's success, producer Reggie Lucas would have been married to Madonna, let alone be working with her again. But of course, the predictably unpredictable starlet moved on to another mentor for **Like a Virgin.** The man she chose this go-round was Nile Rodgers, whom Madonna has described as "a

is on a roll and, while it is difficult to imagine how, both of them promise to get even hotter.

At the MTV video awards, Madonna took the house down with her in-the-flesh prerelease premiere of "Like a Virgin." From her first chime of "I made it through the wilderness" that evening live from Radio City, it was more than apparent that she had outdone herself with the new album. Her vocal talents have grown exponentially, the production is bigger and more lush, the material

stronger and more intelligent. She even has a ballad, "Love Don't Live Here Anymore," that is so beautiful in its sadness that you can understand what she meant when she said that "I'd love to be a memorable figure in some comical tragic way."

Still, her critics abound, reviewing her albums ruthlessly and charging her as a flesh peddler. **Rolling Stone**'s Kurt Loder wrote about "Madonna's bare-bellied, fondle-my-bra image" among other accusations of the old "sex sells" routine.

"I'd love to be a memorable figure in some comical tragic way."

"I find it ridiculous when people accuse Madonna of selling sex," shrugs Michael Rosenblatt, who has left Warner Brothers since signing Madonna and now heads up the talent scouting for MCA Records. "Sex and rock & roll fit together so perfectly that everyone in this business sells sex. Boy George, the Beatles, Elvis Presley, Van Halen, Prince—who isn't selling sex? Maybe Barry Manilow," Rosenblatt laughs, "but that's only because he's after an older market, so he sells love.

"Madonna isn't pushing sex anything like she could if she really wanted to. Her look is a hot 'I'm a 100 percent woman' look, and I think that's great. Rock is full of boys who look like girls and girls who look like boys. Madonna doesn't have to put on black leather and kick the shit out of a motorcycle gang to be cool. I don't understand why people find a girl looking like a girl to be at all offensive. She's not a stripper type, so what's the problem?"

Anyone who has ever known Madonna will tell you that sexuality for her is as natural as feathers are for a duck. Ask any of the tribe of boyfriends she's had in her six years living in New York if Madonna is sexy off camera. If Madonna wore some of the outfits she wears out on the town as costumes on camera, her videos would be censored. "I don't

think I'm using sex to sell myself," Madonna has said. "I'm a very sexual person, and that comes through in my music."

Whatever the price of attracting bitterness, jealousy, and assorted other flak, Madonna stands as an American success story, proof positive that hard work and burning desire are still a combination that can make dreams come true. At 25 she has beauty, talent, worldwide fame, and millions.

The future is blindingly bright for Madonna Ciccone. Even those closest to her who have been predicting her rise to stardom for many years find the reality of just how far she can go a bit overwhelming. As Madonna's first album crossed the 2 million mark, thereby grossing well over $10 million

02:05:20.18

"Lucky Star"

02:03:44.08

"Like a Virgin"

01:33:43.03

01:35:39.16

in American album sales alone, and the release of "Like a Virgin" extended her track record of each single being bigger than the next, it has become nearly impossible to overassess her possibilities.

"Music has gotten very demanding on the young, forming artist," states Michael Rosenblatt. "Imagine a field that asks a young person to master the complex technical and artistic problems of making a record—then expects them to be an actor, too! Yet Madonna masters it all so quickly, so easily, and will increase her audience exponentially with movies, reaching people who might not hear her music.

"I sort of hate to say this," Rosenblatt grimaces at his own assessment, "but Madonna could almost become—wow! I can't **believe** I would say this—but she can become big like Barbra Streisand: a first-rate singer and a box-office draw in the movies. Madonna can be massive in both worlds."

As for the first world, that of music, "can be" no longer applies. Madonna's album **Like a Virgin** debuted at number 70 on the **Billboard** charts released December 1984 and hit number 1 nationally only nine weeks later. Simultaneously, the single "Like a Virgin" was number 1 on **Billboard** charts as well. Madonna's record company actually **plans** to have five singles from the album, all of which will be backed by the-sky's-the-limit video productions. The word on early sales left Norman Hunter, owner of Record Bar, a national album distribution firm, smiling: "To say Madonna (is) exploding out of the box just doesn't do it justice. I'm checking my inventory every half-hour."

Certainly the video for "Like a Virgin," Madonna's most lush production to date, is a plus. The video has a very magical look, thanks largely to its Venice location.

David Lee Roth's birthday party. Flanking "M" are the birthday boy (at left) and Billy Squire.

Madonna showed up at the **Amadeus** party hidden behind a mask. . . .

Traditionally a city of love, Venice was the real-life home of the world's most renowned lover, Casanova.

"We wanted me to be the modern-day, worldly-wise girl that I am," Madonna has said in an explanation of the video. "But then we wanted to go back in time and use an ancient virgin." The action swings back and forth between the two versions of Madonna, depicting her alternately in a nearly sacred long white dress and then as the bare-bellied, gyrating Madonna we have become accustomed to. She chases a man in a carnival mask, and at one point, a lion paces mysteriously in a nearby street. The effect is a dreamlike sense of engaging beauty.

★ ★

By late fall of 1984, Madonna had finished her first movie starring role. The film, directed by Susan Seidelman, was **Desperately Seeking Susan** and co-starred the equally attractive Rosanna Arquette. In the film Madonna plays a wild girl who meets a bored housewife through a personal ad and teaches her how to live in the fast lane. Madonna has said that her role in the film reflected her own personality – "She's

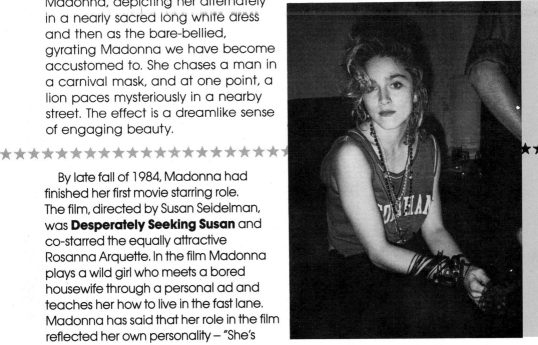

carefree, she's irresponsible – kind of like me."

The film was both a box office and critical success and led to suggestions that Madonna's future lay in film rather than music. Inevitably she was unwilling to be specific. "Movies are just another thing to do," she told interviewers. But she later added that "film is the ultimate thing."

Clearly music was to occupy her immediate future. She recorded three songs as a nightclub singer in the film **Vision Quest** (released in the UK as **Crazy For You**) but only two of them, "Crazy For You" and "Gambler", made the final film. Next she recorded her phenomenally successful second album "Like A Virgin" which contained a slew of hit singles: the title track, "Into The Groove" (which was used in **Desperately Seeking Susan**), "Material Girl", "Angel" and "Dress You Up". No fewer than eight Madonna singles made the British charts during 1985, making her the most successful girl singer ever.

1985 also saw Madonna undertake a large scale tour – The Virgin Tour – opening in Seattle in April and attracting some 355,000 fans in 27 cities throughout the US. Each evening's show was a dance spectacular with Madonna, band and dancers bounding through most of the material from her first two albums. There were costume changes, too, and the finale featured Madonna clad in wedding gown for "Like A Virgin" and "Material Girl".

The tour's itinerary was limited to the USA and the only sour note occurred when the magazines Penthouse and Playboy acquired and printed several photographs of Madonna stark naked, pictures she had posed for while desperate for money in New York at the end of the seventies. "You got paid ten dollars an hour," she recalled when the photos were published. "It was a dollar fifty at Burger King. I kept saying, 'It's for Art.'"

In July Madonna appeared at the Philadelphia Live Aid concert dressed demurely and answering cries of 'Take It Off' with a tart, "I ain't taking nothing off today. They might remember it eight years later." Her Live Aid showcase was characterised by all the pent-up energy of the concerts during her Virgin Tour.

The following month Madonna hit the headlines yet again by marrying actor Sean Penn on her 26th birthday. The news came as a shock – Madonna had

been widely quoted as being against marriage. "The best thing about being single is that there's always someone else. Besides, I wouldn't wish being Mr. Madonna on anybody."

She changed her mind, apparently, in a Tennessee hotel room. "I was jumping up and down on my bed, performing one of my morning rituals and all of a sudden he got this look in his eye and all of a sudden I knew what he was thinking. I said, 'Whatever you're thinking I'll say yes to'. That was his chance, so he popped it."

The ceremony took place on a clifftop at Point Durne in Malibu, California, with the world's press observing from above in helicopters trying to get photos as Sean and Madonna exchanged vows. The razmataz which surrounded the wedding would continue throughout their married life.

Their honeymoon over, Madonna began work on her next album "True Blue" – which would not be released until July 1986 – and then decided that she

and her new husband should make a film together. This turned out to be **Shanghai Surprise**, filmed in England under the auspices of ex-Beatle George Harrison's Handmade Films company, and, like just about everything else associated with Madonna, the filming was conducted beneath a glare of mostly unwanted publicity.

Their problems started when the car in which Madonna and Sean were travelling knocked over a photographer, an incident which received maximum publicity in the UK tabloids the following day and indirectly led to the siege conditions under which filming at Virginia Water was carried out. With photographers and reporters desperate to catch up with them, Madonna and Sean went underground with the inevitable result: bad press. In a belated attempt to clear the air a press conference was held at London's Kensington Roof Gardens with Madonna and George Harrison fending off questions, many of which were deliberately provocative.

"The press are like a bunch of animals, complete animals," said George at one point, while Madonna was asked to apologise for her and Sean's "bad" behaviour. "I have nothing to apologise for," she fumed.

"Everything in the press has been started **by** the press," said George. "Either a photographer sitting on the bonnet of the car, or the girl from Capital Radio who broke in, or the appalling behaviour of one newspaper who stole photographs from the set."

Instead of clearing the air the press conference merely served to exacerbate an already unpleasant situation and the following day's papers unanimously painted a portrait of Madonna as a spoilt child, petulant and pampered, who was unwelcome in the UK. It's unlikely Madonna harboured kind thoughts about England either.

Released later in the year **Shanghai Surprise** was a box office and critical flop, the first failure of Madonna's short career. Reviewers cited a lack of

continuity, poor and unlikely plot development and bad direction as the film's main faults, and Madonna herself made some harsh comments on the film early in 1987.

"I'm extremely disappointed with it," she said. "The director didn't have an eye for the big screen and he seemed to be in a bit over his head. The film company wanted to make an action film like **Raiders Of The Lost Ark** but the script was actually a very personal love story. Unfortunately it was edited as an adventure movie and they left out all the stuff that was its saving grace. We wanted it to be an old romantic movie like **African Queen** and that's what we envisioned when we read the script. It was very hard work doing it so it's a little upsetting.

"They cut all my major scenes down to nothing which made me look like an airhead girl without any character who'd gone to China just on a whim. I also wanted to do a movie that was completely opposite to **Desperately Seeking Susan** where I played a character who was very close to my own personality. I needed a role where I could prove to people that I could really act and that I wasn't just being myself."

Madonna also spoke about the problems encountered while filming in England. "It was like the Third World War," she said. "Sean and I seem to make good press. It's probably because of his reputation of being easily provoked."

Any disappointment felt at the failure of **Shanghai Surprise** was offset by the extraordinary (and simultaneous) success of her third album "True Blue" which shot to the top of the charts across the world and, like its predecessors, yielded several hit singles, all of which were accompanied by interesting – often sexy – videos. To date these have included "Papa Don't Preach", "True Blue" and her most recent 1987 number one UK hit, the Latin inspired "La Isla Bonita".

Maintaining such a high profile –

which Madonna has achieved whether she wanted to or not – has brought attendant problems. Her marriage to Sean Penn is reported to be on the rocks, though she's been quoted as saying she won't divorce Sean because of her Catholic principles. At the time of writing the reality of the situation is unclear: conflicting and dramatic (and probably speculative) stories continue to be written in the popular press as each week rolls by. Madonna is under constant siege from photographers – as is Sean – and it is not surprising that they have adopted an unco-operative attitude towards prying journalists.

Some will consider this to be a small price to pay for the massive stardom which Madonna has achieved. Music industry observers hail her as **the** female star of the eighties, a label that sounds pretentious but is probably an underestimation. With her incredible talent, great looks and boundless determination, Madonna can easily transcend the legacy of any female rock star in the past 20 years.

At 27 Madonna has achieved the ultimate success that the music industry can offer: consecutive multi-million selling albums, starring roles in movies, vast wealth, and the cover of **Rolling Stone**. But in the eyes of Madonna Louise Ciccone, her star has just began to rise. What goals are there left for her to conquer? With a spontaneous blend of defiance, humour and savage honesty, the girl from Detroit declared on American Bandstand: "I want to rule the world!"

Printed in England by Commercial Colour Press, London E7.